# The Human Side
## of Human Beings

### The Theory of Re-evaluation Counseling

*By* HARVEY JACKINS

The Human Side of Human Beings
The Human Situation
The Upward Trend
The Benign Reality
Fundamentals of Co-Counseling Manual
The Postulates of Re-evaluation Counseling
The Communication of Important Ideas
A New Kind of Communicator
The Complete Appreciation of Oneself
Who's in Charge?
The Flexible Human in the Rigid Society
The Logic of Being Completely Logical
Co-Counseling for Married Couples
The Nature of the Learning Process
The Uses of Beauty and Order
The Necessity of Long-Range Goals
Multiplied Awareness
Letter of a Respected Psychiatrist
Is Death Necessary?
The Good and the Great in Art
The Distinctive Characteristics of Re-evaluation
    Counseling
Guidebook to Re-evaluation Counseling
"Quotes"
The Meaningful Holiday — poems
Zest is Best — poems
Rough Notes from Buck Creek I
Rough Notes from La Scherpa I
Rough Notes from Calvinwood I
Rough Notes from Liberation I & II

# THE HUMAN SIDE
# OF HUMAN BEINGS

The Theory of Re-evaluation Counseling

## by Harvey Jackins

RATIONAL ISLAND PUBLISHERS

Seattle

| | |
|---|---|
| First Printing | July, 1965 |
| Second Printing | June, 1966 |
| Third Printing | September, 1970 |
| Fourth Printing | September, 1971 |
| Fifth Printing | February, 1972 |
| Sixth Printing | September, 1972 |
| Seventh Printing | January, 1973 |
| Eighth Printing | January, 1974 |
| First Paperback Printing | September, 1972 |
| Second Paperback Printing | January, 1973 |
| Third Paperback Printing | January, 1974 |
| Fourth Paperback Printing | November, 1974 |
| Fifth Paperback Printing (revised) | May, 1975 |
| Sixth Paperback Printing | December, 1975 |
| Seventh Paperback Printing | August, 1976 |
| Eighth Paperback Printing | April, 1977 |
| Ninth Paperback Printing (revised) | March, 1978 |
| Tenth Paperback Printing | December, 1978 |
| Eleventh Paperback Printing | June, 1979 |
| Twelfth Paperback Printing | April, 1980 |
| Thirteenth Paperback Printing | May, 1981 |
| Fourteenth Paperback Printing | May, 1982 |

ISBN No. 0-911214-60-7 (paper)
0-911214-62-3 (cloth)

Library of Congress Catalog Card No. 65-21901

# The Re-emergent Human

*At peace with all the universe*
*Yet filled with zestful fire,*
*Serene with past achievements,*
*Alive with new desire,*
*Aware of distant galaxies,*
*A pebble I admire.*

*The past informs and reassures.*
*The future beckons bright.*
*I face all human misery*
*And plan to set it right,*
*The genius of humanity*
*A constant, fresh delight.*

*I know the past and plan ahead*
*Yet live the now that's real.*
*I act by thought and logic.*
*I just feel the way I feel.*
*I don't confuse these separate things*
*Nor wind them on one reel.*

*What scars remain from long ago,*
*What fogs still clog my brain*
*Yield to the daily tears and yawns*
*That let me think again.*
*My use of all my gains includes*
*Continual further gain.*

*—Harvey Jackins*

# Contents

# *Acknowledgments*

Gratitude is expressed here for assistance with this book and with the developments of Re-evaluation Counseling theory.

First of all, appreciation is due my family for their participation and support.

Second, appreciation is extended to the thousands of Co-Counselors around the world who have made the goals first written down in the first edition of this book into a reality for themselves and for many others.

# Introduction

This book is an introduction to a theory of human behavior that marks a major breakthrough of human knowledge. It presents a solution to the basic problem of *human irrationality,* a problem which impedes the handling of all the other key questions now facing the world.

Human intelligence is defined concretely as the ability to construct a new, unique, accurate response to each new, unique experience which confronts each human at each moment of his/her existence.

This ability is differentiated explicitly from the ability of plants and animals to "choose" responses from an inherited, restricted list of pre-set response patterns.

Human irrationality is explicitly defined as failure to create and present such a new, unique, accurate response. It is presented as an acquired, non-inherent, unnecessary characteristic of present humans.

The source of human irrationality is located in the distress experiences which the human has undergone and has not been permitted to recover from completely.

The recovery processes, inherent and spontaneous in each human, are retrieved to view from the universal conditioned prejudice which has obscured them and are explicitly presented and described.

Ways of encouraging and assisting these recovery processes to completion and the results following from their use are indicated. These techniques and results are from the counseling practice of the author and his colleagues, a practice set up for the exploration and development of this theory.

This theory of human behavior is in sharp disagreement at many key points with other presently widely accepted theories, but not at any point where these other theories have produced practical results beyond "symptom suppression".

This book is an introduction only. Later publications will deal with the techniques of applying this theory with individual people and groups of people, and with its wide social implications.

Dec. 1, 1964

# The Human Side
## of Human Beings

The Theory of Re-evaluation Counseling

# CHAPTER I

## *What to Expect*

The following is a short description of what a human being may be like, in the important area of the human's response to the environment. It is a descriptive model of what *you* may be like, an attempt at a general guide to understanding all human beings and the source of their apparently contradictory activities.

This descriptive model has grown out of a deliberate and continuing attempt, now fourteen years in progress, to take a fresh look at human beings, to see what they are actually like without assumptions from past theories and models. This fresh look has been difficult to accomplish because of the depth and persistence of the suggestions with which all humans are burdened during our childhood and education years, but it has remained a clear goal during the period this model has been developed.

1

You may find this theory difficult to think about at important points where it is in sharp conflict with the theories you were expected to accept uncritically at your mother's knee, in Sunday school, from your psychology classes or from reading "psychological" fiction. The effort is worth making; these differences from older theories are among the most important things this description has to offer.

These differences require that this description be *thought about*. It cannot be accepted uncritically on the recommendation of any authority because it carries no such recommendation. The theory of Re-evaluation Counseling cannot be of much use to you *unless it makes sense to you!*

If this theory does make sense to you, it can happen that you find yourself uncomfortable about some of its implications, especially if you are a parent. Speaking as a parent, I can only say — "Welcome to the club."

In distinction to this description's differences with older theories, you may find it in remarkable agreement with your own experiences. It has been painstakingly assembled as the summary of actual experiences of hundreds of people.

2

I think you will find this descriptive model to be well-constructed. It assumes or defines a small number of simple concepts and these are related directly to common experiences on which there is general agreement. With these the model proceeds to a useful and consistent explanation of complicated and diverse phenomena.

This descriptive model leads directly to useful activity, to the tackling and solving of human problems, and provides consistent guidance for this activity. It leads continuously to the examination of new questions and to the opening of new fields of thought. New attitudes towards long-unsolved and vexing problems of human behavior, sociology and philosophy can appear as corollaries emerging from the central theses of this model.

You are likely to find this description of a human being useful to you, in the sense that you can cope with and solve certain problems that arise in living better with it than without it.

What follows is an outline of this theory.

# CHAPTER II

## *Life versus Non-living Matter*

This description begins with a comparison of the human's responses to the environment with those of other living things. *The responses of a human being to the environment resemble the responses of other living creatures more than they resemble the responses of non-living matter.*

This may seem obvious, but it is meaningful. Let us look at what we mean.

In general, non-living matter is passive in response to its environment. Give a chair a push and it is pushed. A billiard ball moves away from the cue-ball in a way largely determined by the momentum of the cue-ball, the angle of impact, the elasticity of the materials, etc. The general description of non-living matter's response to the

5

environment is that it is passive, it is "pushed around" rather than "taking charge".*

The distinctive characteristic of living creatures, however, is exactly their *active* response to the environment. Living creatures tend to impose their organization on their surroundings. In the simplest, common-denominator way this is done by consuming a portion of the environment as food and reproducing. Thus a heap of relatively unorganized compost, when exposed to a pair of well-organized earthworms, will become converted in part and in time into a heap of organized earthworms.

Living creatures impose their organization on the environment in other ways besides ingestion and reproduction. The great Minnesota iron deposits, the chalk cliffs of Dover, the coral reefs of the Pacific are all sizeable structures achieved by the active, selective responses of certain microorganisms to the environment. The work of a

---

* (There are beginnings of active, organizing responses to the environment, even in non-living material. A seed crystal, for example, suspended in appropriate solution will "organize" the randomly oriented ions about it into a large crystal patterned after its own structure. Protoplanets will apparently grow into planets by attracting and accreting dust and debris from the primeval dust clouds. This is not the dominant behavior of non-living matter, however.)

colony of beavers can alter profoundly the surface geology of the valley they select for a dam.

Human beings, too, consume part of their environment for nourishment and, by reproduction, convert part of it into new human beings. Our numbers exceed three billion planet-wide. We are, *par excellence,* the living species that pushes the environment around in other complicated ways as well. We mine coal and metal, dam and bridge the rivers, terrace the hillsides, toss satellites into orbit, and prey upon all other species for food, raw material, decoration and sport.

To repeat, human beings are like other living creatures in their active responses to the environment more than they are like non-living matter with its overall passivity to the environment.

# CHAPTER III

## *The Human Difference*

Human beings are *different* from all other living creatures in the *kind* of active responses they make to the environment. What is this difference?

All living creatures with the exception of humans are able to respond actively to the environment only on the basis of *pre-set patterns of response*. These patterns are fixed in the heredity of the individual creature and are very similar to the patterns of other creatures of the same species or strain. The number of available patterns of response may be small for a simple creature and large for a complex creature, but the number of such patterns is finite and fixed in either case. These patterns can become disorganized and damaged during the lifetime of the individual creature, but they will not improve except through a process of maturation which is itself a pre-fixed response. A fine bird dog can have its delicate response patterns ruined by mistreatment, but the dog breeder will not expect better patterns of response than are called for by the particular dog's heredity.

These response patterns are usually called instincts, and the word is a good one if not carelessly applied to humans. When new response patterns do occur in a given hereditary line, this will be regarded as an evolutionary leap, a mutation. It will represent the emergence of a new strain or species.

Since the available patterns of response are fixed and limited in number for any one living creature other than a human, each such creature must categorize, i.e., it must meet a very large number of different environmental situations by lumping together those which are similar and meeting them with the same response. This type of behavior seems to have satisfactory survival value only for the species, not for the individual (speaking statistically).

One can apparently equate pre-set pattern (instinctive) behavior and species survival. When a given species' set of pre-set response patterns works well enough, that species survives. When it does not, that species dies out. Many species of living things have died out in past times and their one-time existence is known to us only by their fossil remains.

This kind of behavior does not carry a very high survival value for the individual. It permits the species to survive only in association with massive reproduction rates.

A pair of codfish are reported to set about 14 million baby codfish adrift on the ocean currents each spawning season. Each of these baby codfish is equipped with the typical codfish assortment of pre-set response patterns. Each is able to respond to the environment only in codfish ways, not in ivy vine ways or butterfly ways.

These codfish response patterns certainly have worked well enough until now that there are still many codfish in the ocean. Yet the individual survival chances of one of these baby codfish would be far from what we would desire for ourselves, since, on the average, only *two* of these 14 million baby codfish survive to be parents of the next generation.

The overall behavior of all forms of life except human can be characterized as active response to the environment, a tendency to impress the surroundings with one's activity, but only on the basis of rigid, pre-set, inherent response patterns which can only roughly approximate the kind of behavior needed for survival in a particular circumstance.

A human being is different. The central feature of our humanness is a *qualitatively* different way of responding actively to the environment. Whether this essential difference was acquired by evolution or by creation makes no difference in understanding and using it.

This "human" ability seems to consist precisely of an ability to create and use *brand new,* unique responses to each new, unique situation we meet. When we are functioning in our distinctive human way we do not have to, nor do we, use any pre-fixed, inherent or previously worked out responses, but always and continuously create and use new precise responses that exactly match and successfully handle the new situation which we confront.

Let us stress this definition. We are not saying that a human being is *quantitatively* more complex in his/her behavior than an angleworm or a dog, in that the human can choose among a larger number of pre-set response patterns than lower animals can. We *are* saying that human behavior is *qualitatively* different than the behavior of other

12

forms of life in that the human being can and does continuously *create new* responses all through the lifetime of the individual.

This essential difference has not been clearly faced in past theories or models. The long, persistent attempts by experimenters to understand human intelligence on the basis of their experiments with laboratory animals, for example, have led to more than one "dead end" school of psychology which explain everything about human beings except our "humanness" and which have been intuitively rejected by thoughtful people because of this.

We usually call this special human ability of ours our *intelligence.* This word is suitable and will generally be understood if we first draw a sharp line, as we have done above, between this flexible, creative, *human* intelligence and the rigid, pre-set responses of plants and animals. Intelligence in our human sense creates an endless supply of new, tailored-to-fit responses to the endless series of new situations we meet.

The behavior called "intelligence" in animals is based on categorizing, classifying and lumping together of different situations which are somewhat similar and meeting them with one rigid, pre-set response.

A moment's thought will make it clear that a human being never confronts an "old" situation. There are no identities in the physical universe, not even two electrons are identical. Certainly anything as complex as an environmental situation for a human will never be repeated exactly.

CHAPTER IV

# The Operational Procedures of Intelligence

This special human ability of ours seems to work as follows:

(1) It continuously receives from the environment a great volume of information, coded in neural impulses, from the excellent battery of sense channels which each human possesses. This vast computer-like ability of ours receives many kinds of visual information from our eyes, many kinds of audible information from our ears and skull bones; it receives taste information, smell information, temperature information, balance information, and kinesthetic information from our many other sense organs.

(2) This vast volume of information coming into our intelligence is continuously and

quickly compared with the information already on file in what we usually call our memory, information from past experiences which we have already understood. Similarities between the incoming information and the information on file are apparently noted, as well as the ways in which similar experiences in the past have been successfully met.

(3) At the same time, this incoming information is *contrasted* with the information already on file; i.e., the differences are noted as well as the similarities. The incoming information is *understood* in relation to other information, in its similarities and differences to other data, not ever as a concept by itself.

(4) The information of how similar experiences were handled successfully in the past is used as a basis for constructing a suitable response to the present situation. The differences between the present situation and the similar past situations are, however, allowed for, and the actual response becomes tailored-to-fit the present exactly, as far as the available information allows.

(5) The new information from the current situation, having now been evaluated in terms of both its similarities and differences to other information, now goes on file in the memory as useful material with which to evaluate later experiences. We are better able to meet later experiences because of what we learned from the previous one. (This effect, for instance, will be very noticeable in beginning a new job in a new field. What is learned in the first week makes the second week comparatively easy to handle.)

This evaluation process is conducted both on aware and unaware levels. Usually the great bulk of evaluation takes place without aware attention, which is reserved for the most interesting or critical information. The assumption made in many theories that awareness and unawareness mark the boundaries between rational and irrational processes turns out to be misleading and is expressly *not* included in this description.

CHAPTER V

## How Much Intelligence?

This ability, this flexible intelligence, is apparently possessed by each of us in such a very large amount as to be difficult for us in our present conditions to envisage.* Apparently if any of us could preserve in operating condition a very large portion of the flexible intelligence that each of us possesses inherently, the one who did so would be accurately described as an "all 'round genius" by the current standards of our culture.

This is not, of course, the impression that most of us have been conditioned to accept. We have heard, from our earliest age, that "Some have it and some don't", "Where were you when the brains were passed out?", "Don't feel bad, the world needs good dishwashers, too," and similar gems. These

---

* This capacity is destroyed or diminished permanently apparently only by physical damage to the forebrain.

impressions and this conditioning, however, seem to be profoundly wrong.  Each of us who escaped physical damage to our forebrain began with far more capacity to function intelligently than the best operating adult in our culture is presently able to exhibit.

The adult who does function extraordinarily well compared to the rest of us, and whom we do call a "genius" in our admiration and respect, seems to be not someone who was endowed with extra ability to be intelligent when the rest of us were "hiding behind the door", but rather someone whom circumstances allowed to keep a considerable portion of his/her flexible intelligence functioning while everyone around him or around her was having theirs inhibited and interfered with.

CHAPTER VI

# A Schematic Diagram

A schematic diagram of this ability can be made by enclosing a large area of paper with a closed curve to represent a large amount, a genius-sized amount, of this ability to think flexibly. *(Fig. 1)*

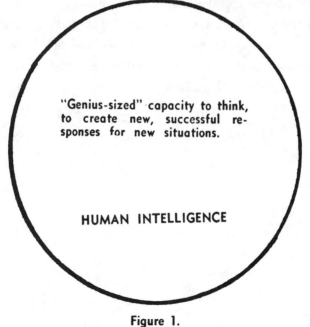

"Genius-sized" capacity to think, to create new, successful responses for new situations.

HUMAN INTELLIGENCE

Figure 1.

We sketch some rectanguloid filing cases around the top and sides of this closed curve. These represent our memory storage. Here the information from good experiences is filed after being understood in terms of similarities and differences to other data. *(Fig. 2)*

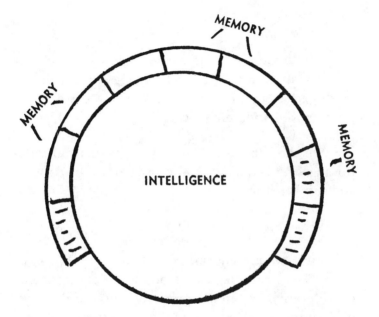

Figure 2.

We locate the environment below the curve in this schematic with a funnel leading from it to the intelligence, and little doorways (our sense channels) in the wide entry. *(Fig. 3)*

On this diagram we will trace the natural functioning of a human and the occurrence of damage and mis-function.

What are we like inherently?

First, we are enormously intelligent. We have a very large capacity to respond to the environment continuously in new, precisely successful ways. This intelligence seems to be the essence of our humanness.

The second essential characteristic is a *feeling* or *attitude*.

*A Schematic Diagram*

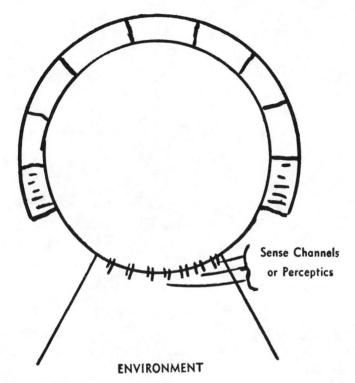

Sense Channels
or Perceptics

ENVIRONMENT

**Figure 3.**

# CHAPTER VII

## *Other Inherent Characteristics*

Apparently, the natural way for a human being to feel is *zestful*. Inherently, a human being "gets a whale of a kick" out of living. He/She views problems as interesting challenges to be solved with enjoyment, not as occasions to be depressed or anxious or irritable.

The third basic human characteristic fits well with the other two. It is the natural relationship *between* any two humans.

This relationship seems to consist precisely of enjoying *affection to* another person, enjoying *affection from* another person, enjoying *communication* with another person, and enjoying *co-operation* with another person.

Vast intelligence, zestful enjoyment of living, loving, co-operative relationships with others — these seem to constitute the essential human nature.

All the rest of human behavior and feeling except these three innate characteristics and their results is acquired, is *not* inherent, is the result of something having gone *wrong*.

All repetitive mistake making, all failures to handle the environmental situation well, all the terrible feelings which enclose adults so much of the time, all the miserable relationships that are common between adults in our societies; all these spring from a single common kind of source.

Something goes wrong.

Certainly, if the above description of what the inherent human is like is valid, something *has* gone wrong. The vast intelligence, enjoyment of living, and excellent relationships with others which we have described as inherent are not in clear evidence in adults.

What goes wrong?

## CHAPTER VIII

# *The Source of Damage*

*We get hurt.*

Just that, *we get hurt.*

Very early in life the first time, and repeatedly after that, we meet experiences of distress. When we meet one — whether the distress is physical (pain, illness, unconsciousness, anaesthesia, sedation, acute discomfort, etc.) or whether it is emotional distress (loss, fright, frustration, ridicule, boredom, etc.) — a particular effect takes place.

*While hurting, physically or emotionally, our flexible human intelligence stops functioning.*

The ability that is the essence of our humanness, our ability to see things as they are exactly and to contrive new exact responses to all new situations, is slowed down or becomes inoperative.

This is a simple, profound and important statement. It is a long-unfaced key to much that has been confusing about a human being's activities. You will find that it sheds light into many dark puzzles about ourselves.

When I and my associates first realized, about two and a half years after we began the work that led to this descriptive model of a human, that we could actually generalize to this point, that we found no data that conflicted with this impression of a general principle, we were very excited.

We have remained excited, as this statement's validity and importance have become more and more apparent. Yet, curiously enough, once seen, this general principle turns out to be part of the intuitive store of knowledge of our population. It reveals itself in descriptive phrases with which we are all familiar and which we all use to describe the effects of a distress experience.

Do these phrases seem familiar to you?

"I was scared out of my wits!"

"She was out of her mind with pain."

"He was so mad he couldn't hit the ground with his hat."

"She seemed to be in a fog for months after her mother died."

"You'd better take the rest of the day off. You're so upset, you'll only make mistakes, anyway."

Give your attention to any one of these familiar statements. (There are many more just as familiar.) Each is a remarkably accurate description of a particular case of the general phenomenon — *we can't think intelligently while we are in distress.*

This is a disadvantage, of course. We would much prefer to have "presence of mind" (note the intuitive accuracy of the familiar phrase) while distresses are occurring.

Temporary loss of intelligence is only the beginning of the mischief, however. Something even more serious and consequential ensues.

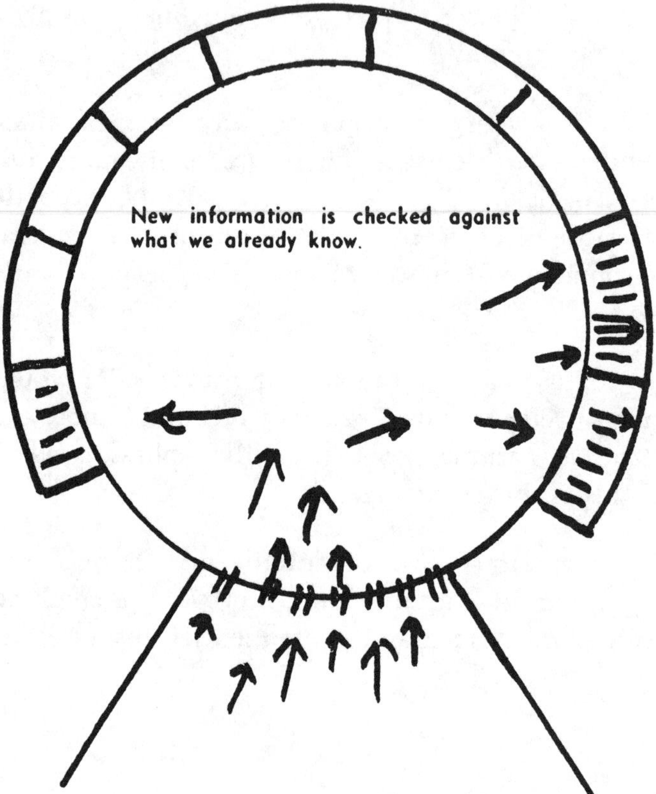

New information is checked against
what we already know.

Figure 4.

# CHAPTER IX

## *The Mis-storage Process*

Though the "thinking machinery" is shut down and inoperative during the distress experience, the information input from all the environment which it usually handles suspends very little, if at all. Information continues to enter the distressed, non-thinking person in great volume through the senses of vision, sound, touch, etc.

This information input during a distress experience stores, or, more correctly, *mis-stores*, in a very different way from the usual information input that we take in during a non-distressing experience.

Information from a good experience becomes useful information which we can use to handle the next experience more "wisely". *(Fig. 4)*

(Incidentally, the usual information storage is done, apparently, in "discrete bits"; i.e., we can remember and use information from a good experience either piece by piece or all together, as we choose.) *(Fig. 5)*

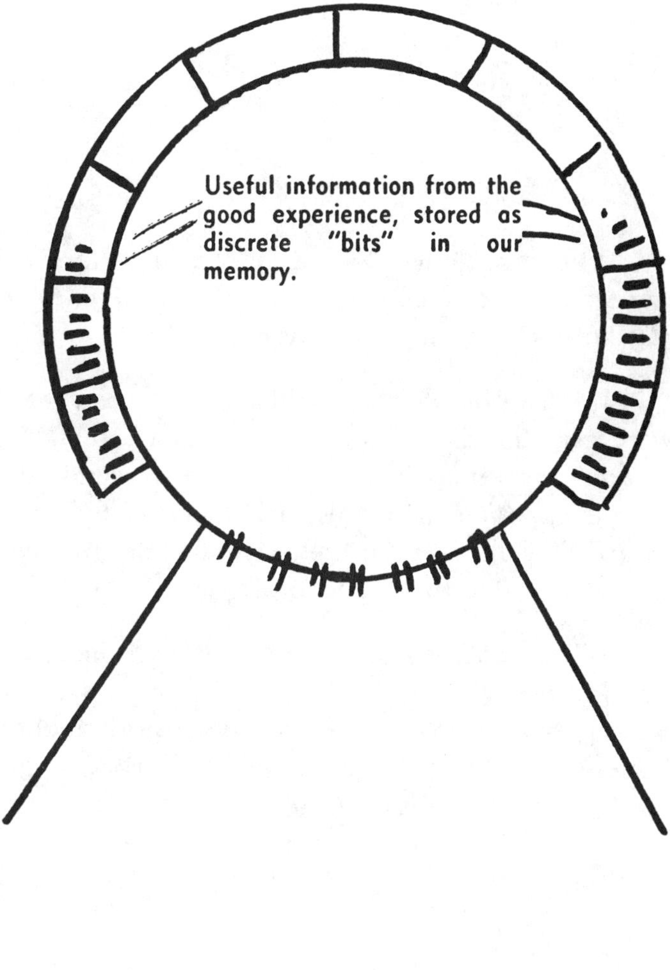

Useful information from the good experience, stored as discrete "bits" in our memory.

Figure 5.

The mis-storage of the information received during a distress experience is very different. It can be described in several ways.

If we think of our flexible intelligence as if it were gear-and-cog computing machinery, then the information input during a distress experience acts as if it deposited onto this machinery *when it was shut down,* piled up on the gears and cogs in a certain area and *jammed them. (Fig. 6)*

When one comes upon this residue in a person's behavior and feelings later, the impression is very much that of a frozen, nonsensical rigidity. Unless the observer knows how this residue got there it seems to make no sense at all.

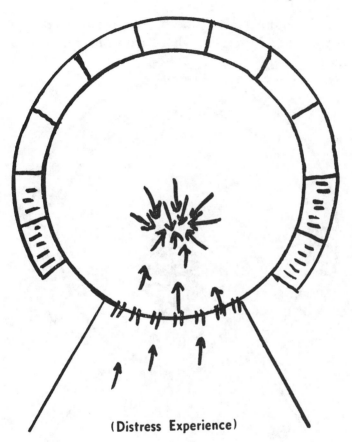

*The Mis-storage Process*

(Distress Experience)

ENVIRONMENT

Figure 6.

37

In another way, this mis-storage behaves as if
it were a rigid scar on what used to be flexible surface. *(Fig. 7)*

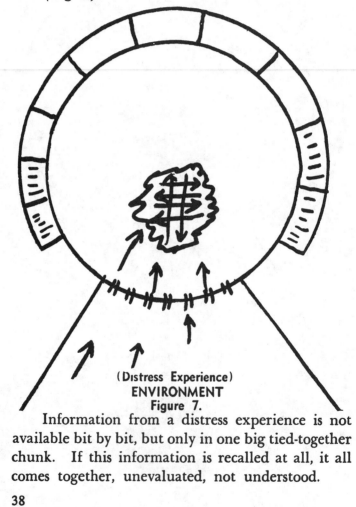

(Distress Experience)
**ENVIRONMENT**
**Figure 7.**

Information from a distress experience is not
available bit by bit, but only in one big tied-together
chunk. If this information is recalled at all, it all
comes together, unevaluated, not understood.

In yet another important way, the mis-stored information input from a distress experience behaves as if it were a recording, a very literal, detailed, complete recording of everything that went on during that distress experience. *(Fig. 8)*

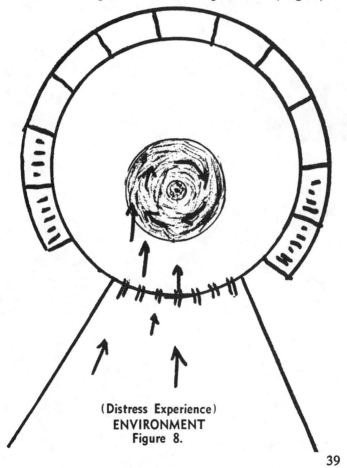

(Distress Experience)
**ENVIRONMENT**
Figure 8.

It is as if the sights, the sounds, the tastes, the touches, the temperatures, the balances and all the rest of the information together with the *feelings of distress and the inability to think* were all recorded simultaneously on one ninety-channel record.

# CHAPTER X

## *The First Bad Effect of Mis-storage*

Most of us have assumed that we were "over" a distress experience, that soon after it had ended we were "back on our feet again". Actually, this should and could take place, and the discussion of how to get it to take place is the main purpose of this book.

Probably because of the way in which human cultures and civilizations have developed, this real recovery from the effects of distress experience rarely takes place.

Instead, the residue of information mis-storage left by the distress experience remains mis-stored. Two important effects result.

The first of these effects is *quantitative*. In ordinary language, we are not as intelligent as we were before the distress experience left this mis-storage upon us. Part of our originally vast, genius-sized intelligence is left tied down, in-operative.

It is not just that there is now a certain area of experience where we no longer think very intelligently. That is true; but there is also an overall lowering of our total capacity to think flexibly, to handle our environment well.

This quantitative effect will not be noticed by us when we are still young. Apparently we have so much more of the capacity available than we usually call upon that we don't miss the lost portion during our youth.

This quantitative effect will be noticed later in life, however. As many distress experiences accumulate and are re-inforced by re-stimulation (which we will discuss later) the growing *lack of capacity* to think may be noticed.

We might call the noticing point "middle age", although it arrives in the teens for some and in very advanced years for others. Many persons seeking help describe this lack spontaneously in their initial interview.

"I'm losing my grip" is a favorite description.

"Running out of slack" is another common one. "These last years seem to have taken all the starch out of me," said one person. "I'm not the man I used to be and I'm beginning to think I never was," said another. "I don't seem to have what it takes any more" is common.

These descriptions are quantitative in nature and express awareness of a loss of ability for coping with the environment. This first effect, the quantitative loss effect, will not be noticed in youth.

# CHAPTER XI

## *The Second Bad Result*

The *second* kind of effect will be *noticed* while young, but not *understood.*

The second kind of effect can be examined by viewing the distress mis-storage as a recording. Carrying this distress-experience recording, we are now "booby-trapped".

*When we are confronted by a new experience that is similar enough to the recorded distress experience we are compulsively forced to meet it with an attempted re-enactment of the old distress experience.*

One might say that, "reminded too much of" the old distress experience, we are forced to behave as if we were some kind of walking "juke-box". In effect, the new experience "pushes the button". The recording of the old, miserable experience then rolls out as if from a rack onto a "turntable in our head". The recording now *plays us*! *(Fig. 9)*

The person now in the grip of this recording of an old distress experience says things that are not pertinent, does things that don't work, fails to cope with the situation, and endures terrible feelings that have nothing to do with the present. This is sub-human behavior, quite unlike the creative, capable behavior of a thinking person.

We are all familiar with these occurrences as we observe them in other people, though we have not understood them. We can almost (almost!) say that we have never had any trouble with another human being except for just this sort of occurrence; i.e., except for the irrational way people behave when they are upset.

Otherwise, we get along fine with everyone, don't we?

The "almost" above allows for the times when *we* become upset and we behave irrationally. We can accept the existence of such times logically, but we are not capable of observing them at the time.

The experience which "reminds us too much of" the old distress experience and thus triggers the

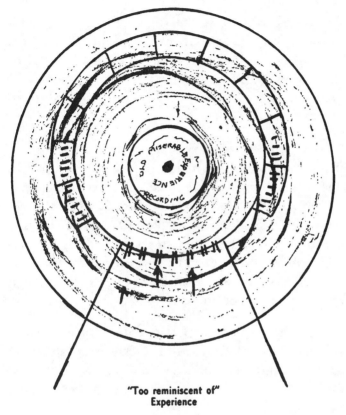

"Too reminiscent of"
Experience

ENVIRONMENT

Re-stimulated, the distress recording "takes over", dominates the behavior of the person, compels an attempted "re-enactment" of the original distress experience.

Figure 9.

47

distress recording into "taking over" may be itself a distress experience. It may contain occurrences intrinsically distressing to us. This may be one of the strong points of similarity to the old one. *It does not, however, have to be intrinsically distressing to have this effect.*

All that is necessary is that it be *similar enough* in enough ways, that it smell enough like the old one, have enough of the same voices, colors, characters in it. When this requirement is met, then distress feelings indistinguishable to the person feeling them from current ones are supplied by the re-stimulated recording. The present experience feels and affects us like a distress one, even though perfectly innocent in its actual content.

In the grip of the re-stimulated distress recording, the person talks foolishly, acts inaccurately and unsuccessfully, and feels terrible feelings that have no logical connection with what is actually going on.

## CHAPTER XII

# The "Snowballing" of Distress

This distressed behavior is bad enough. It is, however, not the last of the mischief. The "thinking machinery" is inoperative once again. Once again information is fed through the sense channels to an intelligence that isn't functioning.

The information input from this new experience is new. It cannot be evaluated, however, while the rational processes are interrupted. *This information input also mis-stores in the same way as the original distress experience.*

The effect is as if more random, unevaluated debris clogs more areas of our thinking machinery. One might say that "more gears are jammed", or that "the booby trap acquires more triggers", or that

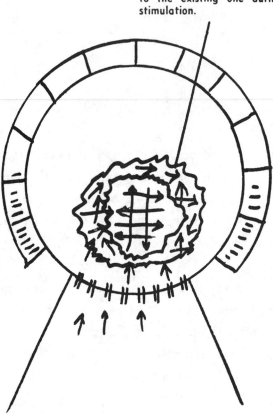

Additional patterns of rigidity, added to the existing one during its re-stimulation.

Figure 10.

"the ten-inch recording grows to a twelve-inch one".
*(Fig. 10)*

The net effect is that each experience of being re-stimulated or "reminded too much of" in this way leaves the person *predisposed* to be upset more easily, by more things, more often, more deeply, and for longer periods of time.

The effect is a snowballing one. It is as if the hurt patterns were sticky surfaces which attract and add new sticky surfaces at a geometric rate.

## CHAPTER XIII

# *The Early Beginnings of Damage*

Each of us, of course, meets hurt experiences very early in his/her life. Our physical weakness, lack of experience and information and the resulting extreme dependence on others when we are very young leave us wide open to be hurt repeatedly in this period.

These early hurts may be inflicted by many things. Bumps and bruises and accidents and cold and hunger and frustration can all play their part.

In our civilization, however, the dominant source of hurts when we are very young is precisely the distress patterns of the adults around us. For an adult to behave irrationally *is* upsetting to a baby; and when that irrationality consists of or is accompanied by crossness, reproach, invalidation, ridicule, aloofness or violence as it usually is, the hurt is severe.

53

Perhaps you can imagine an infant playing happily with her mother. She is warm, happy, outgoing, loving towards her. The mother is warm, happy, outgoing, loving to her baby. The world is a wonderful place.

Then the phone rings and the mother goes to answer it. Baby waits for the wonderful play to resume. She has no way of knowing what signals come to her mother over the phone, nor of understanding their effect if she did know. So it can happen when the mother returns and baby stretches her arms to her warmly and lovingly, she is met with an expression of disgust and a loud, harsh voice saying "Don't bother me!" in tones of hate.

Sounds coming over the phone have triggered an old distress recording in the mother, which takes over and "plays" itself at the baby through her. The source of the recording has nothing to do with the baby or the mother's relation to her. Baby, however, *is hurt*, and a recording etches itself as she stops thinking and the experience mis-stores.

Whatever distress the experience contains will remain rigidly attached to the entire experience and to any experience which "reminds" the baby of it later. This rigid effect will vary greatly with each infant, depending on details and especially on what earlier distress patterns already exist to be re-stimulated by this one.

One infant in a situation like the above may be left with a fixed distrust of all other people. Another may be left with a rigid sense of his/her being a "bother".

In any case, the "tracks" of this kind of early experience will show, with great effect, among the rigidities of the adult into which the infant grows. The adult, in his/her first interview with a counselor, is likely to volunteer that he/she "is a nuisance", that he/she wants help to quit being "such a bother to everybody". A host of later distress and/or re-stimulation experiences will be related as indicating what a "bother" he/she is, but eventually, as his/her counseling progresses, the effect of the early experience will emerge as the significant "direction-fixer" it has been.

We are hurt early and often, primarily by the distress patterns of the adults in whose charge we are. These early hurts are re-stimulated and added to at an increasing rate, becoming chronic and "numb" (i.e., seeming to become calloused) in some areas, but always continuing to clog our thinking abilities at an increasing rate. *(Fig. 11)*

This is the bad side of "growing up". This process of "ossifying" our flexible intelligence has gone on relentlessly for all of us.

The snowballing process, as distress patterns predispose more distress experiences.

**Figure 11.**

CHAPTER XIV

## *The Extent of the Adult's Loss*

The degree to which this limiting process has gone on is something we have been slow to face. In the first years of our work, we did not suspect either how intelligent humans are to begin with or how severely that intelligence has been interfered with for any adult. We can only estimate now, but we can make an informed estimate.

We estimate that the *successful* adult in our present culture, the man or the woman whom everyone would agree is doing "just fine", is operating on about ten percent of his or her original resources of intelligence, ability to enjoy life and ability to enjoy other people.

The other ninety percent of her or his vast potential is covered over with rigid patterns of behavior and feeling, the mis-stored information

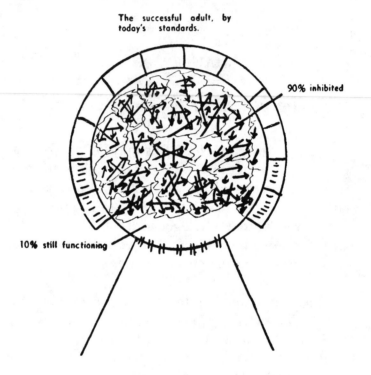

The successful adult, by today's standards.

90% inhibited

10% still functioning

Figure 12.

residue of unevaluated experiences of distress. *(Fig. 12)*

Most of these patterns are *latent,* i.e., they behave as if they were recordings waiting in the rack. They inhibit the human's capacity and lower his/her potential, but they do not dominate his/her behavior nor his/her feeling except and until they are re-stimulated by particular circumstances in his/her environment. These recordings do not play until he/she is "reminded too much of" the distress experience.

It is easy to think of examples from your own experience. For many people, a "stage fright" recording only takes over when the particular conditions of the public appearance re-stimulate it. Most people do not go around "stage frightened" all the time. Many spouses only "go to pieces" a certain way when under the critical scrutiny of a parent-in-law. They do not feel nor act irritably defensive in that particular manner at other times.

CHAPTER XV

## How Distress Patterns Become Chronic

For all of us adults, however, a few distress patterns have been re-stimulated to the point of becoming *chronic*. These have become, in effect, recordings which play all of the time.

The chronic patterns can be described in various ways. It is as if the push button for these recordings was pushed so often it broke in the ON position. It is as if these recordings finally "built their own turntables" and play all the time. It is as if the person has made some kind of surrender to these particular patterns.

The chronic pattern is worn by the individual as if it were a portable prison cage. He/She remains rational, flexible, and intelligent only in ways that

**63**

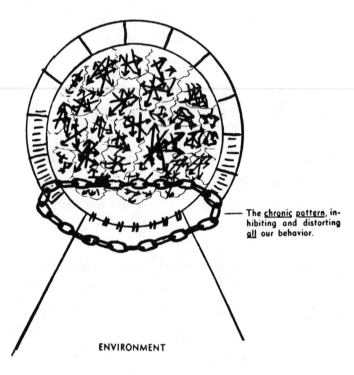

The <u>chronic pattern</u>, inhibiting and distorting <u>all</u> our behavior.

ENVIRONMENT

Figure 13.

do not contradict the chronic pattern. *(Fig. 13)*

We view our own *latent* distress patterns as difficulties, as "problems", if we are aware of them at all. The chronic pattern will, on the other hand, be defended by the wearer as the "only way to be" if it is called in question. We defend these chronic behaviors and feelings if they are held up for discussion. We compulsively and unhappily regard them as our "personalities" or, at worst, "interesting idiosyncrasies".

Permissive counseling will not suffice to undo a chronic pattern, though it is usually quite sufficient for a latent one. Much more resource, time and ingenuity will go into unraveling a chronic pattern and freeing the wearer from it than are necessary for a latent one. The counselor needs to be equipped with a thorough understanding of the difference.

Chronic patterns become very "total" in their effect upon their victims. They are manifested in postures, repetitive cliches of speech, rigid rituals of behavior that are included in the responses to all situations. They include chronic emotional attitudes. These emotional attitudes will become etched upon a person's facial expression in the signs of grief, anxiety, etc., which most older adults wear whenever in "repose".

Yet chronic patterns arise and have their sources in exactly the same occurrences as the lighter or "latent" patterns. Each is the residue of unevaluated experiences of distress acting as compulsive recordings of behavior and feelings. The chronic recording simply plays all the time once it becomes re-stimulated past a critical point.

# CHAPTER XVI

# *A Rational Explanation for Irrational Behavior*

In this collection of distress patterns, latent and chronic, which has accumulated on each human lies a simple and adequate explanation of "what is wrong with people". The infinite variety of "bad" behavior and distress on the part of people becomes the literal and unavoidable result of the infinite variety of ways in which we humans are hurt. What is "wrong" with a particular person is a unique thing, the unique result of the unique distress experiences which he/she has endured and mis-stored, experiences which never exactly happened to anyone else.

This understanding immediately makes unjustifiable many old unworkable approaches to human misbehavior and distress. Punishment, reproach, shaming, ostracism, isolation, condemnation or enforcement have never worked well in dealing with human problems. Thoughtful observers of human relationships have noted this many times but have not succeeded very well in interrupting the quantitative practice of them in society.

The understanding of the distress recording mechanism developed above makes plain *why* these old approaches cannot work.

We do not have human beings with *inherent* conflicts which they must learn to live with; we have consistent human beings warped into apparent self-conflict by *acquired* distress patterns which act contrary to their inherent rational nature.

We do not have *bad* people; we have *good* people acting bad when they are short-circuited by the emotional scar tissue which has been loaded on them by the environment.

We do not have people who *purposely* do wrong; we have non-survival behavior enforced upon *innocent* humans by the unhealed residue of damages done to them. We do not have mean, destructive, vicious humans; we have kind, constructive, loving humans *compelled* to mean, destructive, vicious behavior by unhealed distress of which they are the first victims.

We are not surrounded by un-understandable creatures, forever beyond effective contact; we are among people just as good as ourselves who can be understood easily where they are rational and whose distresses can be understood and *gotten rid of* where they are irrational.

We do not have a warped species of creatures who are inherently bent on mutual destruction; we have a divinely gifted species who create art, music, science, and beauty and make no negative moves except when "turned off" and acting as puppets whose strings are pulled by old scars of hurts, either of their own, or ones that have become congealed in a rigid social structure and culture.

## CHAPTER XVII

# *Open Doors for the Child*

From this follows a most important possibility. *People do not have to become hurt and irrational.* Children can be protected from most experiences of distress and helped to free themselves from those that do occur. It is possible for children to remain their real selves. Children can be allowed to grow up and become adults and yet remain the happy, loving, successful geniuses that they are inherently.

This is simple and clear even though it will not be easy to accomplish. We adults do not begin the change with a fresh slate. There is no one to take charge of, care for, and look after the children except us adults, and all of us are severely distressed and conditioned to pass similar distresses along to the children, even though we have the best intentions in the world.

The general trend of human progress is with

us. The level of irrational behavior is lower as the generations pass. With many irregularities, people are acting more rationally, more human, are treating each other and their children better as the years go by.

This encouraging reality should not be obscured by the fresh outbursts of horror and discouragement emitted by viewers who panic as they take their first aware looks at how bad things are without comparing them with how bad things have been in the past. The trend toward being more rational is unmistakable in human history and human society, even though it is very uneven.

There is even clear indication of *acceleration* in human improvement, with only present mechanisms in operation. Many thoughtful people are aware of this. Their alarm has attached itself to the possibility that the improvement will be too slow to prevent social irrationality and hydrogen bombs from exploding together.

There is progress in human affairs; yet the almost systematic transmission of irrationality from generation to generation goes on. An "intelligence from Mars" might well view the people of Earth as explorers have described some remote and primitive tribes all of whose members are ill with malaria.

Sick all of their lives, it is difficult for these tribes-people to imagine what it would be like to feel well. It seems "normal" to them to drag through marginal lives, able to wrest only the scantiest of livings from the environment, and too miserable to enjoy what they do secure. Each child is born healthy, with a full potentiality for a good, rich life, but, immediately infected with malaria by the environment, the child soon succumbs to illness and drags through the rest of his/her life at the level of the rest of the tribe.

The "observer" from Mars might see Earth's people as they are, inhibited by the distress and irrational behavior patterns they assume are "normal", seldom suspecting their own true capacities. The Mars person might see Earth's children as they really are, born with tremendous capacities for mastering their environments, for enjoying themselves and for living well together, but quickly infected with the same kind of distress patterns which infest the adults, and in due time growing into "typical" irrational adults.

Even the beginnings of understanding as to how humans are hurt can make a decisive difference in how much distress loads upon our children. Parents who understand these mechanisms theoretically will still feel pressure to be "upset" at their children but they can resist that pressure to a great degree, and their children will respond to the difference very noticeably. These parents will know what is going on when children begin to discharge spontaneously after a hurt and will let them cry (or shake or laugh or storm) at least part of the distress out even though they still feel the conditioned urge to make them stop.

Enough parents have spent enough time by now trying to apply these principles to make it clear that even small efforts in this direction show up in impressive differences in the children. In happiness, in school work, in attitudes to others, in intelligence and creativity, these children who have been partly protected from hurt and allowed to unload these hurts that occur show a clear gain over their companions whose parents have not understood.

# CHAPTER XVIII

# *The Recovery Process*

The last few paragraphs have anticipated the most important and essential part of Re-evaluation Counseling theory: *The process of damage and loss caused by distress experiences can be reversed and the lost intelligence and abilities can be recovered.*

Human beings are equipped inherently, not only with vast intelligence and capacity to enjoy life and other people, not only with the susceptibility to having this endowment damaged and limited, but are also equipped with *damage repair facilities,* healing processes. These processes undo the effects of hurts immediately after the hurts happen, they remove the stored distresses immediately after they occur *whenever they are allowed to work.*

These damage repair processes, at least the outward manifestations of them, are very familiar to all of us. Everyone has experienced them and has observed them *but all of us have been so thoroughly conditioned that it is very difficult for us to think about them, especially when they are present and operating.*

To think about these fundamental healing processes, consider a new, unconditioned human being, an unhurt infant. Consider this infant to be in a very special environment. This environment is to consist essentially of caretaking adults who are so free from the usual accumulation of hurt patterns that they are able to be relaxed and undistressed when the baby is distressed, that they will not become upset by the baby's upsets.

Adults so free from rigid reactions towards a baby in distress do not exist, at least in noticeable numbers, in our general population. All of us have accumulated too many hurt patterns by the time we are adults. Nevertheless, this condition has been approximated by adults who have freed themselves of substantial quantities of their accumulated distresses through Re-evaluation Counseling. The overall description of what happens will not be hard for the reader to credit because it will fit his/her own experiences.

If this new, still human baby who has these

relaxed adults in his surroundings happens to meet an experience of hurt, the process of hurt storage takes place as we have described. Let us suppose that he loses his mother in a crowded downtown street for about ten minutes, and that this is a deeply distressing experience even though a short one. Let us further suppose that Mother returns at the end of the ten minutes, that the bad experience as such is ended at this point.

Now if Mother is as we have hypothesized — relaxed, aware, attentive, and undistressed — if she gives to the baby her aware attention and concern, gives him her arms and eyes but *keeps her mouth shut* and does not talk, sympathize, jiggle, distract or interfere, then the damage repair process of the baby goes into action. Without hesitation, spontaneously (no one has to tell the baby what to do) he turns to this attentive mother and begins to cry. Allowed to do so, he cries and cries and cries and cries. He will continue to do so for a long, long time if every time he slows down and looks out at his mother he finds her still interested, still attentive, still caring, *but not interfering or distracting*.

He will cry and cry and cry for what will seem to be a very long time and then he will be done, really done. Now the baby will change remarkably. He will resurge to obvious happiness, to great enthusiasm and alertness, to awareness and outgoingness and activity. This process is very exciting to observe. The freshly discharged child is an impressive picture; one feels as if the clouds have parted for a moment and the real human being is showing through.

Apparently the profound healing process of which the tears are the outward indication has drained the distress from the mis-stored bad experience residue and the baby's mind can now get at the information itself, perceive what actually happened, and finally evaluate it, make sense of it, understand it. The mis-storage becomes converted to ordinary information, is stored correctly, becomes available to help understand later experiences with in the usual way. The rigid responses which had been left by the bad ten minutes are gone. The recording is no longer available to be triggered by later incidents. The frozen portion of the baby's mind is free to work again. *(Fig. 14)*

You can check the alternative from familiar experience. If the baby does not get a chance to cry thoroughly enough and get the bad experience "out of his system" completely, his mother can expect the upset recording to be triggered the next time she tries to leave him with the babysitter. If

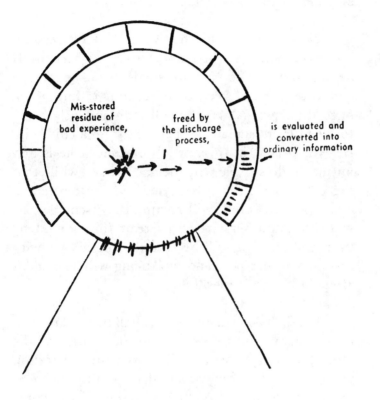

Figure 14.

he did cry out his distress thoroughly right after the bad experience, her leaving him next time will be taken in his calm stride.

Now consider another variety of distress experience. Suppose the baby is badly frightened. If he has someone to turn to who is able to be relaxed and attentive and keep from reacting to him, then, once the fright is over, he will spontaneously begin to tremble, to scream, to perspire from a cold skin. He will persist in this for a long time if he is permitted to do so. He will check once in a while that the other person is still paying aware attention to him, and, reassured, will resume the discharge. He will shake and perspire and scream for a long, long time and then he will be through. Again, as with tears, great alertness and well-being will be evident after the trembling is all done.

If a baby is frustrated (and all babies are frustrated many times every day in the course of the usual handling), she will discharge the frustration and get it out of her system if she is allowed to do so. If someone will really listen, she will discharge in what is usually condemned in our culture under the name of "tantrum". She will make violent physical movements and angry noises, and will perspire from a warm skin. This is exactly what she needs to do.

80

If the person present with her will hear her out, fully and with attention (undoing or removing the source of the offense first, if possible), she will go on yelling and flailing and perspiring for a long time. It will seem even longer to an embarrassed parent, particularly if it happens in public. If she is allowed to do so freely, however, and is not again frustrated in the effort to quiet her, she will come to the end of this discharge also and will emerge a relaxed, happy and co-operative child.

The child, who has been ridiculed or made to feel embarrassed in some way (and we all had this done to us many times when we were young) and then can turn to the relaxed, interested adult we have described, will seize the opportunity to talk to the adult about the embarrassing experience. If the adult listens with attention and keeps her advice to herself, the child will narrate the embarrassing experience repeatedly and will finally attempt to joke about it. Soon, she will begin to laugh. She will laugh harder and harder as she returns to her narration. Finally, having laughed out her tension, she will walk completely free from the embarrassment that had gripped her to the point that she was afraid to face her associates.

# CHAPTER XIX

## *What Has Kept the Recovery Processes from Operating*

All of us discharge in these spontaneous ways in the beginning. It is our nature to release like this after every hurt, to turn to another person and let go, to get the hurt out of our system. Every unconditioned baby does this with precision and vigor when he/she is allowed to do so.

None of us *were ever allowed* to do so to any great degree. Why were we not?

We *had* to turn to someone. The process does not work well at all for one person alone. It requires the aware presence of another person to proceed to completion.*

---

* Fairly recent reports in the "Scientific American" indicate that this requirement is pre-human. In one article, baby Rhesus monkeys are reported to be unable to overcome fear of new playthings unless they have at least a soft, substitute mother of terry cloth upon which they can clutch and rub and squeak for an

So all of us turned to another person as we began the healing discharge of, say, our tears. When we did, the sound of our crying became a "button pushing" re-stimulation of that person's mis-stored distress. As infants we had no way of knowing that this person was not, properly speaking, rational Mother or Dad or Aunt Sally any more. Each kept the appearance of our familiar adult ally. They were not any longer thinking rationally, however, for at this point each became functionally a robot being played *by* an old distress recording and playing an old recorded announcement *at* us.

In one family, the recorded announcement may go something like this: "There, there, don't cry, it's all right, don't cry. (Jiggle, jiggle) There, there, don't cry, don't cry, don't cry."

You have heard others which go: "All right, son, get a grip on yourself! No use crying. Crying doesn't do any good. No use crying over spilt milk. All right, now! (etc.) ."

Other varieties which have been observed and

---

extended period of time. Another article reports that baby sheep who are hurt with electric shock remain neurotic in their behavior as a result if they are denied access to and physical contact with their mother. If they are allowed to rub against and bleat to their mothers they appear to make at least a large measure of recovery.

reported include: "Shut up! You stop your crying or I'll give you something to cry about." "Please stop crying, you're making Mama feel bad." "Look, see the pretty picture. Isn't it nice? It's more fun to look at a pretty picture than it is to cry, isn't it?"

Whether kindly or cruelly in word or tone, each of us was made to turn off our healing processes, while we were hurting. Usually, the one reproach did not keep us from trying to release the next time we were hurt; but, inexorably, the same thing happened. Each time we turned to someone and began to discharge and get rid of our hurt, we were told, apparently by the adult to whom we turned, that we must not discharge, that we should suppress our feelings and hold them inside ourselves.

These recorded patterns of interfering with another person's discharge of their distresses (for that is what they are) are passed on from generation to generation by a kind of contagion. Our entire culture is soaked in them. The great majority of lullaby lyrics contain "don't cry". Up to now the obvious wrongness and harmfulness of suppressing emotional discharge has not penetrated the pervasive conditioning caused by these recordings. Occasionally people who have actually tried to help distressed people have been forced to realize this.

They have gone against the conditioning enough to write articles saying that it is helpful to cry. No one, to our knowledge, has followed up these beginnings enough to realize that this suppression of discharge is the basic reason why our entire population is so troubled, so unable to live up to their potentials.

One can observe very small children trying repeatedly to let go of their feelings and being repeatedly made to choke them back. As they grow older, they appear to shut off their own discharge as the shame and embarrassment conditioning takes over.

## CHAPTER XX

# *People Never Stop Trying*

Yet we do not ever really give up trying to get our hurts out of our system, not even as weary adults. The more we observe people with these insights in mind, the more it is clear that each person, every day of his/her life, reaches out to someone in some way or other. He/She makes an intuitive attempt to set up with this other person the relationship he/she should have had with his/her parents when he/she was small and the need of which he/she has carried with him/her ever since.

This applies to all of us. Sometimes we "bend the ear" of the casual stranger, sitting beside us on the bus. Sometimes the housewife in a new neighborhood systematically invites every woman on the block in for coffee, and asks back the one who seems willing for the conversation to be two-way, to listen as well as be listened to. We cherish the friend we can "talk" to, or think we can. We lean on the minister of our church in crises, and jam the waiting rooms of the medical doctors with vague, psychosomatic complaints which might open the way for the doctor to really pay attention to us. We marry, often or always, with the unexpressed hope that this time our beloved will "care enough", though we are too conditioned to be able to look at what their "caring enough" is supposed to do. Our most bitter disappointment, expressed over and over again in marital interviews, is that our spouse "doesn't listen" or "isn't interested".

All of us feel deeply this need of our own to have someone listen to us, to pay real attention to us, to care about us, but all of us are thoroughly conditioned to refuse to meet this need in others.

On occasion a woman may turn to another woman in a crisis and burst into tears and, since women are not as badly conditioned in this area as men in our culture, be offered a shoulder to cry on and even told "Go ahead and cry, dear, it will do you good." If she ever begins to cry as hard as she needs to, however, the conditioning will be triggered and, at the least, the other woman will begin to pat her so hard with reassuring pats that the distraction will make it impossible for her to keep crying.

A man may, in a crisis, turn to a friend and say, "Look, Joe, I've got to talk to somebody!" and begin to tremble violently. The friend, thoroughly conditioned, is almost certain to do everything he can to interrupt the trembling. "Here, man, get a grip on yourself! I'll get you a drink, you've got to stop this shaking." If he isn't a drinking man, he may call in a doctor to stop the shaking and the doctor, just as conditioned as all the rest of us, obligingly may give him a shot or a sedative. "Anything to stop his shaking."

Yet it is obvious, if we are not at the scene, that the man is shaking because he needs to and that nothing bad will happen if he is *allowed* to shake until he runs down.

At the scene, the conditioning takes over and the acquired compulsion to stop the discharge (as our own was always stopped) takes over and drives all rational considerations from view.

Usually our attempt to set up this relationship doesn't get as far as actual release. The attempt usually begins conversationally.

"Hey, Joe," says the friend at the picnic table. "Did I ever tell you about that time some of us were camping up in the North Woods and we were portaging our canoe around this little series of waterfalls?" The speaker at this moment has no awareness at all that he is doing anything but trying to entertain his friend with an amusing anecdote.

He has no awareness at all that he is trying to get to the end of the story where the canoe went over a waterfall and he thought he was dead, the part where a chunk of cold horror has been stored inside ever since, seeking a chance to discharge.

Most likely he never does find out what he is trying to do. As soon as he pauses for breath in his conversational preface, his listener, himself re-stimulated by the story, is likely to break in, "It's funny you should bring that up. It reminds me of the time when I was camping up north, blah, blah, blah...."

Typically the first man can't listen to the second man's story either. The relationship fails for lack of an aware listener on either side. Both men are frustrated in their attempts.

We continually seek this concern and attention from others, even though we are continually disappointed. I have on occasion asked a lecture audience, "What would it be like to have someone really, deeply interested in you and wanting to hear you talk about yourself indefinitely?" A deep, yearning sigh always goes up from the audience, before the realization of what they have admitted triggers embarrassment and the following burst of laughter.

We intuitively hope for this relationship from our spouse when we marry. Each spouse feels the need of it from the other. "I thought, when you married, your husband would care enough about you to be interested in you" is the disappointed, bitter complaint in marital interview after marital interview. Yet each spouse, *hoping* for this aware concern from the other (even though he/she does not awarely *expect* the emotional discharge that would occur if he/she were to receive it), is also thoroughly conditioned by the distress recording to *not give* this concern to the other. This disappointment and bitterness is a major component in the difficulties that, small or great, accumulate in every marriage relationship.

# CHAPTER XXI

## *The Process Works for All*

The damage repair facilities do not ever become destroyed, apparently, short of physical damage to the forebrain and/or other organs involved, though they become very inhibited by the distress patterns themselves, especially those of the "Don't cry" variety.

The damage repair processes are specific in character, dependably characterized by the outward manifestations of 1) crying, 2) trembling, 3) laughing, 4) anger discharge, 5) yawning and 6) interested, non-repetitive talking. These damage repair processes, allowed to operate and assisted to operate, restore the adult to intelligent, zestful functioning just as they do the infant or child, no matter how long the adult has carried the distress.

There is much more accumulated distress to discharge in the adult than in the child. The discharge processes will be more hindered by the distresses themselves in a typical adult than in a typical child. Nevertheless, the processes themselves work as well and have the same results in adults of any age as they do in children or infants.

We do not yet know if an adult, or, for that matter, a child, can fully and completely recover *all* of their inhibited intelligence and zestful capacity for living. We have not yet reached this point with anyone, though it has been a theoretical goal from the time that we began to realize the implications of the discharge and re-evaluation process. Neither, however, are there any indications in theory or practice that this complete recovery will not be possible. It appears that we have simply not reached this point in the evolvement and practice of Re-evaluation Counseling at the present date (1964).

We did not realize at first what a tremendous amount of distress has accumulated upon each person. Partly this was because there was no available starting point or yardstick to measure this accumulation against. We had no example of an undistressed human with which to compare the rest of us. All adults, and, to a lesser degree, all children, were already carrying a large amount of inhibiting distress.

The goal of total awareness and complete rationality is a real one for all of us who have used and enjoyed the benefits of Re-evalution Counseling in any continuing manner. There seems to be no reason why complete recovery should not be possible. The process certainly accelerates as it is applied, with larger gains being made more easily as the functioning capacities of the human emerge.

Aside from the question of complete recovery, each step a human takes in this direction is satisfying and worthwhile. Each gain in rationality is a gain in our enjoyment of living. The achievement of short-range goals and progress towards long-range ones becomes a dependable process. Awareness of one's environment and enjoyment of it becomes better and better instead of fading as it does for the typical adult. Relationships with other people become more enjoyable and productive. Our children have better models to learn from and more intelligible sources of information and show it promptly in their flourishing progress.

# CHAPTER XXII

## *Learning to Use the Theory*

As is surely plain to the reader by now, Re-evaluation Counseling is a relationship that can be used by any person, both as client and as counselor. A very deeply distressed person will need help as a client for some time to begin with, but, given such help, can then learn to be an effective counselor also.

Two people can "take turns", *A* being counselor to *B* at one session, but later taking a turn as client while *B* is counselor. Such "co-counseling", as we have called it, requires awareness and persistence and willingness to apply counseling to difficulties as they arise. It can be very effective and become increasingly so. The interchangeable relationship is itself very rewarding and illuminating.

To learn to counsel or to co-counsel requires

an opportunity to learn. The opportunity to date has been largely in the Fundamentals of Co-Counseling Classes which we have conducted. There have been several score of these classes — two to four months in length — on a one-session-a-week basis.

In these classes, lectures on theory alternate with demonstrations on counseling, with a willing student serving as demonstration client. Students pair off for co-counseling outside of class, report on and discuss their co-counseling in class. Almost all of the successful counselors, who constitute the "rational island" community today, began in these classes.

But not all. Counselors isolated by geography from the Seattle groups have in increasing numbers trained their own co-counselors in the communities to which they have moved, have enlarged their circles, and established co-counseling groups.

To date, success as a counselor has proceeded from success at *being counseled* in almost every case. Not surprisingly, the experiencing of the discharge and re-evaluation process and its results is the factor that illuminates one's allowing and encouraging it to take place in another person.

There is a great deal to learn in becoming an effective counselor, but people are eager, willing, and able to learn rapidly, also. Being counseled, observing counseling in demonstrations, practice as a counselor, discussion, and persistent encouragement and reassurance from an experienced counselor have seemed to be decisive factors in effective learning.

# CHAPTER XXIII

## *Looking Ahead*

To date several hundred people have learned to use Re-evaluation Counseling with consistency. These people tend to think of themselves as inhabitants of a "rational island" of humans which they are helping to pull up out of the sea of irrationality in which people and civilization are struggling.

Most of these "counseling people" live in and near Seattle, but there are a few on each continent and in many states. They apply Re-evaluation Counseling in their personal and family relationships, deal skillfully with their associates at work and exchange assistance with each other as they need it.

The existence of this group has great meaning for the future. The spreading use of their relationship can eventually cleanse the human community of petty antagonisms and misunderstandings which are today such a burden to the lives of everyone.

The gradual improvement in the lives of each generation of children can be accelerated into great strides forward in each generation. Thoughtful acceptance of and participation in the rational use of our wonderful planet for the benefit of all can become part of every human's life. The great irrational threats to human existence of war, prejudice, overcrowding and starvation can become relegated to the role of historical curiosities, much as we think of cannibalism and human sacrifice today.

We have seen clearly what human beings are intended to be like. We have seen a significant number of humans emerge decisively into this kind of living and behavior. The aware, effective goodness of the real human being will inspire any person who has once glimpsed it to take the workable path of discharge and re-evaluation on the way to a bright future for the individual and the race.

CHAPTER XXIV

## *After Thirteen Years*

On the occasion of the thirteenth reprinting of this book, thirteen years after its first publication, it is perhaps proper to inform the reader of the progress of Re-evaluation Counseling in the intervening years.

When *The Human Side of Human Beings* was first published, almost all of the people who used Re-evaluation Counseling lived in or near the city of Seattle, Washington, where the work began. Chapter XXIII speaks of "several hundred" participants. That has changed greatly.

Today (January, 1978) there are sizable, organized groups of Re-evaluation Co-Counselors in forty-five of the fifty United States, in seven Canadian provinces, at scores of locations in the United Kingdom, in both the Republic of Ireland and Northern Ireland, at five locations in Australia, and in one or more communities in France, Italy, Switzerland, Germany, Belgium, The Netherlands, Norway, Sweden, Denmark, Poland, Greece, Israel, Mexico, Colombia, Peru, Argentina, Guatemala, and Hong Kong. Hundreds of thousands of people participate in Re-evaluation Counseling regularly.

There are now special publications for black co-counselors, for Latino co-counselors, for Francophone co-counselors, and for classroom teachers, physically different persons, religious workers, mental health workers, American Indians, Asian-Americans, college and university faculty, social activists, young people, older people, parents, wage workers, Jews, women, song writers, poets, and health workers.

*The Human Side of Human Beings* has been translated into French, German, Dutch, Danish, Spanish, Norwegian, Swedish, and Esperanto. It is presently being translated into Hebrew, Chinese, and Japanese.

The theory has developed greatly in these years. Many other books, pamphlets, and periodicals have been written and published carrying the theory and practice forward from the brief introduction presented in this book. As an introduction, however, *The Human Side of Human Beings* remains sound and satisfactory. We have, on two occasions, swept through it to eliminate the sexist use of male pronouns as a common gender, which has so long been endemic in the English language, but that has been all the revision needed.

It continues to be a pleasure and a satisfaction to read and re-read, not only for its author, but for many, many people for whom it first opened the doors to a much more meaningful and satisfactory life.

# The Author

Harvey Jackins was born in Idaho, grew up in Minnesota and Montana, and attended the University of Washington, where his major interests were chemistry, music, and mathematics.

His first dozen years after college were spent in political activity and as a labor organizer. In this same period, he attracted some attention as a poet and an inventor.

Accidental circumstances confronted him with the problem of distressed human behavior in the early 1950s. The successes and insights which led to Re-evaluation Counseling followed. A private corporation — Personal Counselors, Inc. — was organized to carry on counseling, teaching, and research in 1952.

Since 1970, the ideas of Re-evaluation Counseling have begun to have world-wide impact. "Communities" of co-counselors have formed in most population centers of the United States and in many other countries. Much of his time is now spent traveling, conducting training workshops, and lecturing. He is the designated International Reference Person for the Re-evaluation Counseling Communities. Persons interested in being in contact with these practicing groups of Re-evaluation Co-Counselors are welcome to write to him at 719 Second Avenue North, Seattle, Washington 98109, U.S.A., for information.

Besides *The Human Side of Human Beings*, he has written *The Fundamentals of Co-Counseling Manual* (1962), *The Human Situation* (1973), *The Guidebook to Re-evaluation Counseling* (1975), *Quotes* (1975), *The Upward Trend* (1975), *The Benign Reality* (1981), and two books of poetry, *The Meaningful Holiday* (1970) and *Zest is Best* (1973), all published by Rational Island Publishers.

# RE-EVALUATION COUNSELING PUBLICATIONS

The Human Side of Human Beings — *Harvey Jackins*
Fundamentals of Co-Counseling Manual — *Harvey Jackins*
The Human Situation — *Harvey Jackins*
The Upward Trend — *Harvey Jackins*
The Benign Reality — *Harvey Jackins*
Guidebook to Re-evaluation Counseling — *Harvey Jackins*
"Quotes" from Harvey Jackins
Zest is Best. . . Poems — *Harvey Jackins*
The Meaningful Holiday. . . Poems — *Harvey Jackins*
The Postulates of Re-evaluation Counseling
The Communication of Important Ideas — *Harvey Jackins*
The Complete Appreciation of Oneself — *Harvey Jackins*
Who's in Charge? — *Harvey Jackins*
The Flexible Human in the Rigid Society — *Harvey Jackins*
The Logic of Being Completely Logical — *Harvey Jackins*
Guidelines for the Re-evaluation Counseling Communities
Co-Counseling for Married Couples — *Harvey Jackins*
The Nature of the Learning Process — *Harvey Jackins*
The Uses of Beauty and Order — *Harvey Jackins*
The Necessity of Long-Range Goals — *Harvey Jackins*
Multiplied Awareness — *Harvey Jackins*
Letter to a Respected Psychiatrist — *Harvey Jackins*
Is Death Necessary? — *Harvey Jackins*
Permit Their Flourishing — *Staff of Palo Alto RC Pre-School*
A New Kind of Communicator — RC Teachers' Outlines
The Distinctive Characteristics of Re-evaluation Counseling —
*Harvey Jackins*


Rough Notes from Buck Creek I
Rough Notes from La Scherpa I
Rough Notes from Calvinwood I
Rough Notes from Liberation I & II

*continued on next page. . .*

## CASSETTES OF LECTURES BY HARVEY JACKINS

An Introduction to Re-evaluation Counseling
Loneliness and Learning in San Luis Obispo
Social Change
Affection, Love and Sex at the University of Maine
The Importance of Policy and Theory *(Side A) and* A Tentative
    Policy on Anti-Semitism *(Side B)*
The Oppressive Society
How RC Started *(Side A) and* Radio Interview at Arlington, Va.;
    Discussion with Dr. Morris Parloff and Staff at NIMH *(Side B)*
The Basic Skills of Being a Counselor *(Side A) and* The Inevitable
    Stages in the Development of Co-Counseling *(Side B)*
The Spectrum of Techniques
Leadership *(from a Reference Persons' Workshop)*
Comment Commença le Coconseil — *Translated by Daniel Le Bon*


## VIDEOTAPES

Discharging The Patterns of White Racism
Reclaiming Our Power
Challenging the Chronic Pattern
Counseling on Classist Oppression
A Young Person's Challenge to Adultism
Counseling on Sexist Oppression
Counseling the Rape Victim
Counseling on the Patterns of Anti-Semitism
A Rational Policy on Sexuality
The Origins of Classist Oppression and the Remedy
Counseling on the Patterns of Homosexual Oppression
Counseling on Physical Hurts
The Oppression of the Physically Different


*For additional information and price lists, write to:*

RATIONAL ISLAND PUBLISHERS
P.O. Box 2081, Main Office Station
Seattle, Washington            98111

## NON-ENGLISH EDITIONS

| | |
|---|---|
| CHINESE: | Fundamentals of Co-Counseling Manual |
| DANISH: | Det Menneskelige I Mennesker |
| | Handbog Genvurderingsvejledning |
| DUTCH: | Handleiding voor de Beginselen van het Co-counselen, Voor Beginnersklassen in Re-evaluation Counseling |
| | Het menselijke aan de mens |
| ESPERANTO: | La Homa Flanko de Homoj |
| FRENCH: | Le Côté humain des Etres humains |
| | Manuel Élémentaire de Réévaluation par le Coconseil |
| GERMAN: | Die Menschliche Seite der Menschen |
| | Handbuch für elementares Counseling |
| GREEK: | Fundamentals of Co-Counseling Manual |
| HEBREW: | Fundamentals of Co-Counseling Manual |
| JAPANESE: | The Human Side of Human Beings |
| PORTUGUESE: | O Lado Humano Dos Seres Humanos |
| SPANISH: | El Lado Humano de los Seres Humanos |
| SWEDISH: | Handbok I Omvärderande Parsamtal |
| TELEGU: | Fundamentals of Co-Counseling Manual |

## PERIODICALS

Asian-American Re-evaluation
Black Re-emergence
The Caring Parent
Clarity
Classroom
Colleague
Complete Elegance
Creativity
Directory of College Faculty in RC
The Elders Speak
Forever and Ever
Foundation Journal
Growing Older
Handicapped, but Not Incapable
Heritage
Lawyers RC Journal
Men
Our Asian Inheritance
Pensamientos

Present Time
Priests' and Nuns' Newsletter
Proud Allies
The RC Teacher
Recovery and Re-emergence
Réémergence
Respect
Ruah Hadashah
Seeds and Crystals
Sisters
Songs On Our Way Out
Sunrise
Transcendence
Upcoming
Well-Being
Wide World Changing
Working for a Living
Young and Powerful

# WHAT SOME PEOPLE HAVE SAID ABOUT
## "THE HUMAN SIDE OF HUMAN BEINGS"

"This book introduces an extremely original and powerful approach to understanding and improving human behavior. I consider the author to be a genius of the first rank whose ideas are rapidly becoming influential on a world wide scale."
— Prof. Thomas J. Scheff, Chairman
Department of Sociology
University of California
Santa Barbara, California

———————————— • ————————————

"Quakers believe that there is 'that of God' or 'an inner light' in every person. Quakers have often been frustrated by human behavior that hides that light. Re-evaluation Counseling points the way toward permanently uncovering the loving, co-operative goodness in each of us. Harvey Jackins' book has opened the door for many of us to the real beauty of our human brothers. The practice, using his techniques, keeps the door open."
— Barbara Taylor Snipes
Morrisville, Pennsylvania

———————————— • ————————————

"Here we have an exciting breakthrough to fresh ideas concerning the nature of man and the path to human fulfillment. The book is lucid, indeed deceptively simple, in that a complex and profound theory is developed in a fascinating and eminently readable manner. This is a work of scientific importance which every thoughtful person can understand. . ."
— John Saunders
Professor of Philosophy
San Fernando Valley State College

———————————— • ————————————

"Here we have a book which faces the essential nature of persons and comes up with reasons why we act as we do. I urge everyone to take time to read "The Human Side of Human Beings" . . . It is especially timely for parents! . . ."
— Reverend George Poor
Riverton United Methodist Church
Seattle, Washington

———————————— • ————————————

". . . . Lucidly written and well organized. It contains a wealth of testable hypotheses for the research-minded clinical psychologist studying psychotherapy . . . . radically humanistic as well as practical. I recommend it, especially for all of us in the helping professions."
— Bernard J. Somers, PhD
Professor of Psychology
California State College at Los Angeles.